# The Book of Lions

## Dr. Diana Prince

AuthorHouse™
1663 Liberty Drive
Bloomington, IN 47403
www.authorhouse.com
Phone: 1 (800) 839-8640

Published by AuthorHouse 07/10/2019

ISBN: 978-1-7283-1859-2 (sc)
ISBN: 978-1-7283-1860-8 (hc)
ISBN: 978-1-7283-1858-5 (e)

Library of Congress Control Number: 2019909250

Print information available on the last page.

PHOTOS:

The Cover Photo and the photos on pages 3, 7, 9, 21, 23, 29, and 33 are used with permission of Getty Images.

All other photos are property of the Author.

This book is printed on acid-free paper.

authorHOUSE®

# Table of Contents

# List of Photos

# Introduction

Lions are members of the large jungle cats, which also include such animals as tigers and leopards. Once common in many parts of the world, lion populations today are drastically reduced.

Lion fossils recovered in Tanzania date back 1.5 million years.

This book explores their family groups, habits and hunting skills.

Their majestic stride and powerful bodies have earned the lion the title of "King of the Jungle."

# 1   The World of the Lion

The scientific name and classification of the lion is "Panthera Leo". The name was introduced by German Lorenz Oken about 200 years ago. Today they exist primarily in parts of Africa, with the greatest concentration in Kenya and Tanzania.

The genus classification "Panthera" includes the other large members of the jungle cats, such as the leopards, tigers and jaguars. Their common ties and divergent development originated as far back as three million years into the ancient past. This was determined by scientific findings that attempted to trace their common ancestry groups.

Lions were once more common throughout Asia, the Middle East, Europe and North Africa, and even in North America.

They were depicted in cave art dating back almost 19,000 years. There are ancient hunting scenes of humans, armed with raised spears, pursuing the great animals thousands of years ago.

At Olduvai Gorge, made famous by the husband and wife research team of Mary and Louis Leakey, some of the finest examples of lion fossils were unearthed. These fossils, unearthed in the region of Tanzania, date back about 1.5 million years.

The lions, with their royal stride, striking manes and powerful bodies, have come to be symbols for strength. Often called the "King of the Jungle", the lion has been used on national flags and royal crests to symbolize the power and might of the world's greatest civilizations.

## 2  Size

Of all of the types of big cats, the lion is the second largest jungle cat after the Tiger. The male lion is significantly larger than the female. Generally the males range between 330-550 pounds. The significantly smaller females weigh between 265 to 400 pounds. The greatest recorded weight of a lion was over 800 pounds.

The normal body length of the lion ranges from four to six feet. There have been rare reports of lions with a body length of ten feet. The tail of the lion will vary from 25 to 40 inches.

Surprisingly, by the time lions are only two years old, they have reached sixty percent of their full adult size. By this time, they are usually already strong and skilled hunters, and ready to set out on their own. When they have reached an age as young adults, the young female lions will continue to live in their same group or "pride". The young males, however, upon reaching early adult hood are forced to leave their group, and establish a new group elsewhere after finding new females to form that group. Sometimes, they are able to become part of another already established group. Their status in the new group depends on the relations already established in that group.

One of the largest lion species was the "American lion" or "American cave lion." It once occupied North America in what is now both the United States and Canada. It is believed to have reached nearly ten feet in length, and to have exceeded a weight of 1,000 pounds. Lions are believed to have also lived as far south as the now frigid fjord areas of remote Patagonia in what is now South America. Many perished in the great glacial period.

# 3  Lion Groups

The lion is considered a very social animal in his relations with family, and his regular interactions with them. The living group of a lion is called a "pride". It ordinarily is headed by two or three male lions, however, this can vary. Several females and their related cubs also make up this familial group.

There are usually between sixteen to twenty lions in a pride. However, in some cases the pride may even include as many as 30 or 40 individuals. This, however, would be the exception.

The makeup of the pride changes over time when the cubs reach their early adult status. At that point, the young females will remain in the group. Over time a group of related female family members endures, including many generations.

However, the young adult males will be forced out of that original group, and will need to establish themselves in new groups where they join other existing prides, or create a new pride with other females. Often, when this transition takes place, especially if other young cubs are a part of that social group, the new males may kill the young cubs in order to father their own new cubs.

Surprisingly, it is the females who do most of the hunting. While the females hunt, their male counterparts guard their territory and ensure the safety of the youngest members of the pride. Male lions survey their territory and protect it fiercely. In some instances, they will be called upon to ward off intruders and to protect the offspring.

# 4  Where Lions are Found

The swaying grasslands and savannahs are a preferred habitat of lions. Today, lions are found primarily in Africa, mostly in regions south of the Sahara. Most lions are found in Kenya and Tanzania in East Africa. Kenya is believed to have approximately 2,000 lions. In the South, the lions are concentrated in Zambia, Botswana, Zimbabwe and the nation of South Africa.

The Hwange lions near Zimbabwe have nearly 2,400 lions. They also occupy the waterways and wetlands in the region of the Okavango Delta. Other lion groups roam in the dry regions of the Kalahari Desert in Namibia. Another 700 lions are in the South African region of Kgalagadi.

The Serengeti National Park in Tanzania is home to one of the greatest concentrations of lions in all of Africa. There are also other large populations of lions in parts of Nigeria and Ghana.

Some safari lodges, such as the one at Chobe, are based primarily for "observation only", with an emphasis on hosting tourist groups rather than hunting parties. This is critical in several places since lion numbers are being so quickly depleted.

In Angola, the law strictly prohibits hunting for lions. Unfortunately, hunters and poachers continue to defy such laws, and local governments continue to enforce laws to secure the safely of the threatened lion population.

In the United States, the Mountain Lion is found in several regions. This lion, found in North America, is often referred to as a "cougar" or a "puma".

# 5 Hunting

Interestingly, it is the female lions who band together and in concert to bring down larger prey. Wildebeest, gazelles, zebra, and other large game are hunted in groups.

One erroneous belief is that humans are the prey of lions. This, however, is untrue. If lions are startled or ambushed by humans, human death may result, but man is not a natural target of the lion.

Hunting can take place from morning to night if circumstances warrant it. However, most hunting is done by the female lions during the evening, depending on circumstances and the availability of food. The lions are adept hunters. Each claw of the lion is about three inches in length.

While females are engaged in hunting for food for the group, males patrol territories in which the pride lives. That area can cover over 80 square miles. While the females hunt the males are on the lookout for other animals invading their territory.

Leopards and hyenas are serious enemies of the lion, and post a great danger. The leopards are particularly dangerous to the lion because of their great size. Hyenas also present a serious threat to lions because they often hunt in large packs, and have powerful jaws. The hyenas often prey on cubs who are left unprotected.

The roar of the adult male is so powerful, that it can be heard at great distances. It is believed that the lion's powerful roar can sometimes be heard from a distance of over five miles away.

# 6  Habits

Unlike many other cats who pursue their activities at night as "nocturnal" animals, the lions can also be very active during the day and are primarily "diurnal". They do, however, take frequent "rest breaks" during daytime hours, often sheltering themselves near trees and shady spaces, as a respite from hot, dry climates.

However, the lion is very versatile and can adapt well to night hunting, if forced to do so by circumstances.

Male lions sleep an average of 20 hours during the day or evening. They often sleep several hours after they have consumed a large amount of food.

The males will often mark their territory with their urine as a deterrent to intruders.

The lion's sense of smell is very acute, which is an asset in hunting. It is also an advantage in being able to detect the presence of unseen predators.

Also, the lion's sense of hearing is much more acute than that of human beings. He can actually hear the movement of his prey from a distance of over a mile.

Surprisingly, despite their considerable weight, lions are very good swimmers.

Lions have been known to kill cheetahs and leopards, but will very rarely eat them. It is not known if this is simply due to the animals being competitors in the food chain.

# 7 Diet

Lions have a large number of targets for prey. They hunt antelopes, rhinos, hippos, crocodiles, buffalos, zebras and giraffes. However, lions will also eat smaller more vulnerable animals such as rodents, lizards, turtles and birds.

Giraffes can powerfully injure lions with their long and strong legs, so lions will generally set their sights on the youngest giraffes, especially if the young giraffes are left unprotected.

The first things that the lions consume when they eat larger animals are the heart, kidneys, and liver which provide the greatest nourishment.

It is typical for the adult male lions to eat first after a kill has been made. The females will eat only after the male lions have eaten. The final meal is eaten by the young cubs.

A female lion will devour 11 pounds of meat in a 24-hour period, with the male lion eating even more. The male lion averages, according to some reports, 20 pounds of meat each day.

Lions are able to consume a huge amount of food at one time, and store it for some time internally if necessary. This helps in a situation where the lion's next meal may be delayed for a significant period time. Sometimes, after consuming a large meal, a male lion will sleep 18 hours straight.

An interesting fact is that a lion can go almost a week without drinking water. This is offset by the blood and moisture in the foods lions consume from their victims.

# 8  Reproduction

The female is able to breed several times during a year. However, she will deliberately avoid breeding until her current offspring reach the age of two years old. The male takes only a few seconds to mate, and can mate 100 times in one day.

The gestation period of development is about 115 days. About two to three offspring are born. The newborn cubs weigh about three pounds. Their mother provides them with milk for the first six months of their life. By the time they are three months old, they will begin to consume meat. Over half of the cubs do not survive for a year.

The offspring are usually hidden or concealed after birth. It is not until they are about six weeks old that they are introduced to the rest of the pride, and become a part of the community. The new cub is called a "whelp", or sometimes a "lionet". Young lions do not roar until they are about one year old.

Within the pride, the females usually give birth during the same time period, based on their shared mating season. These females are usually related, since younger females stay in their original lion family group. Because of this, the females are usually related as daughters, sisters or aunts. They raise their offspring in a communal way, caring for one another's offspring, as well as their own. The young ones will sometimes nurse, after birth, with another related female such as an aunt as well as with their mother. The males, however, are usually forced to leave the group when they reach two years of age. They then will form a new group or enter an established group.

# 9  The Mane of the Lion

The elegant mane is one of the male lion's most pronounced and memorable features. A male's mane begins to grow when he is about 18 months old. It will continue to grow until he is about six years of age.

A darker mane indicates an older individual. The thickness of the mane, the size and the color are often considered features that attract a female lion to the male lion, particularly with respect to mating. However, the mane, with its great thickness, has another purposeful use. It protects the lion's neck in a fight with other male lions and also in attacks from predators.

While most lions have manes with golden, or honey brown shades of coloring, there are exceptions. A unique lion with a noticeable black mane lives in Ethiopia, primarily in the remote mountainous regions. However, not all male lions have manes. A notable exception would be the male lions of Tsavo in Kenya, who have no manes.

There are also rare cases where lionesses have developed manes. English researcher Geoffrey Gilfillan reported such a phenomenon with five lionesses in the Okavango Delta region of Botswana. ("Five Wild Lionesses Grow a Mane and Start Acting Like Males", by Karl Gruber, New Scientist, Sept. 23, 2016). This growth of the manes in the females is a rare occurrence which causes them to emulate some male behaviors. The phenomenon is associated with larger amounts of testosterone in the older female lions. Similarly, in incidents where castration occurs, male lions lose not only their ability to produce testosterone, but also lose their manes.

# 10 The Tail of the Lion

The tail of the lion has several important uses. The tail of the adult male lion is usually between 24 to 40 inches in length.

The lion uses its tail to communicate. When a lion flicks its tail, it is a warning to keep others away. The lion's tail can also be used for balance and for jumping.

The tail is also used to give signals to other lions nearby during the hunt, when audible noises would scare away the prey. The female can communicate to the other lions to signal a warning or a strategy of attack.

The tail is also used to give other signals, including giving communications and directions to the lion cubs. When the female raises her tail, it is a signal for her cubs to follow her.

Unlike the tails of other members of the cat family, there is a sharp, usually black "tuft" of hair at the end of the tail. This covers a sharp bone. It is actually a claw-like shape which can inflict serious harm on enemies when the lion uses it to strike with great force. This bone at the end of the tail can be snapped sharply enough to seriously injure an adversary during a fight.

The lion's tail can also give a silent sign to communicate and alert the other lions of the presence of nearby danger.

Unfortunately, among the reckless souvenir hunters and certain tribes, possessing a lion's tail as a trophy continues to lead to senseless killing of the magnificent animals.

# 11  The Eyes of the Lion

Lion cubs are born blind. They do not open their eyes until several days after birth, usually averaging about six days. When the cubs are born, their eyes are a gray-blue color. Within their first few months of life, their eyes change color and acquire a brown and sometimes golden hue. Lions have a second eyelid, which acts as protection. It is also used to better cleanse the eyes.

Also, lions are not able to move their eyes from left to right easily, and therefore they must move their entire head from side to side in order to see in both directions.

Lions are able to dilate and enlarge their pupil to a greater degree than human eyes. The pupil of the lion's eye is three times the size of the human eye. The eyesight of the lion is almost nine times sharper than our own.

Lions do not have as many "cones" in their eyes as humans, and therefore cannot see colors as well. They primarily see colors in greens and blue. On the other hand, they have excellent vision at night. They have a special membrane which allows faint peripheral light to reach their retina, redirecting it and amplifying it for sharper vision. This especially enhances night vision.

In the retina of the lion's eye, there are photo receptor cells which are extremely light sensitive. This means that they require eighty percent less light to see, compared with the human eye. The bright white exterior markings, underneath the lion's eyes, also reflect additional light into his eyes.

# 12 Life Span

Generally, the life expectancy of male lions in their natural habitats averages 12 years, while females have an expected lifespan of about 15 years. This applies whether they live in savannahs or grasslands. However, in captivity, the average lion lives about 18 years, and can sometimes live as long as 28 years in captivity.

Two thousand years ago, over a million lions occupied the Middle East, India, Europe and other parts of the world. Now they are primarily concentrated in a few parts of Africa, and world lion populations suggest that there may be fewer than 30,000 worldwide. Their disappearance in great numbers over the past fifty years, suggests that they are headed for extinction. Man's reckless hunting has created this situation. Over 600 lions are slaughtered by trophy hunters each year.

One of the rarest and most magnificent of all lions is the "Barbary Lion", also known as the "Atlas Lion", believed to be the largest lion to ever live. They were kept in the palaces of the Moroccan kings. Today the only remaining thirty-two of these lions in the world are in the Rabat Zoo in Morocco. They are the last remaining lions of this sub-species. No others are believed to exist in the wild.

These lions once wandered freely in the Atlas Mountains of Morocco and Algeria, but have now been "extinct" in the wild since the 1960's. The last known Barbary Lions to be kept in zoos included one living in the London Zoo in 1896 and one living in the New York Zoo in 1903.

# 13 Speed

The speed of the lion is generally faster than either the leopard or the tiger. Lions tend to run in short bursts of speed. They will often stealthily approach their prey, so they are not seen. This element of surprise will startle the target, and the lion will then chase after him at astonishing speed.

It is during this pursuit of their prey, that the lions run in short bursts of high speed. In hunting, the female lion runs faster than the male, due to her lower weight. Her normal running speed is about 52 miles per hour, which is about 35 percent faster than the male.

Therefore, while the greater weight of the males is an advantage with respect to strength and sheer power, it becomes a liability when it comes to running swiftly and pursuing their prey. This lesser weight of the female may also be an advantage with respect to jumping. It is believed that the female is sometimes able to jump a distance of over 30 feet.

An interesting situation is that of the crocodile and the lion, who are both fierce adversaries. There is an interesting dichotomy. If they are both on land, the lion will prevail because the crocodile cannot move quickly enough on land. However, if they are in the water, the crocodile is better able to maneuver, and the lion has little chance of escape.

The speed and cunning of lions in rural Africa result in attacks on cattle, even though it is not their preferred food. This makes them targets of local farmers whose livelihood is threatened by the raids on their livestock.

# 14 White Lions

One of the most unique types of lions in the world is the "White Lion". This rare lion is found mostly in a specific area of South Africa called the Great Timbavati, located near Kruger National Park. Most of these lions are protected in reserves.

This rare white lion was first sighted this century in the late 1930's. Scientists have determined that a genetic mutation occurred, and discounted a theory that the rare color was simply the result of an albino gene, with an absence of color.

Biologically, two lions with regular brown or tan coloring are able to be parents to a white lion, if each of them possesses a recessive gene with this property. In any case, the occurrence of such a birth remains a rarity.

There are believed to be fewer than 300 white lions existing in the world today. Only about ten of these lions currently exist in the wild.

Due to their rare and unusual color, they were long sought after by trophy hunters. This hastened their demise.

Today, most of the existing white lions are living in captivity, and they are dependent upon special programs and zoos which are attempting to save the vulnerable white lion population.

Four white lion cubs were born in 2015 at the Toronto Zoo. Other zoos have had some success as well, but not enough to replenish the population.

Two of the oldest white lions are "Gracious", age 17, and "Prosperity", age 20, who are residents of the Cincinnati Zoo.

# 15 Endangered Status

A century ago, there were 200,000 lions in the world. Today experts estimate that their numbers have been reduced to only about 30,000.

Some researcher estimate that in nearly 24 African countries, lions have become extinct. These are astonishing numbers and present a concerning situation.

Today, only about 28,000 lions remain in the wild. About 500 of these lions are in Asia. In the last three decades, the number of lions has decreased by nearly 40%, a shocking statistic that put the animal on the seriously endangered list.

Out of control hunting is one factor. But development of some rural areas has led to a loss of their former habitats as cities and towns expand and extend into undeveloped territory.

This has led to more stringent enforcement of hunting regulations, and to the setting aside of protected areas for this amazing animal.

In Namibia, livestock are often the targets of lions. Cows and other domestic animals such as goats were very frequent targets of lions who often raided local villages and small farms. The government intervened with programs to facilitate ways in which the villagers could co-exist with the lions. Fences and other deterrents were erected with the cooperation of the small farmers and villagers. This consistent effort to coexist is both a government and a local priority in Namibia. To further curb the situation, some lions were also transported to other regions of Africa as a part of this effort.

# 16 Breeding in Captivity

There is a great deal of disagreement regarding the raising of lions in captivity. Some animal activists believe that animals cannot be raised domestically and then be thrust into the wild and survive optimally.

The South African Predator Association, also known as S.A.P.A., believes that lions can be raised and nurtured in captivity, and be successfully introduced into the wild. They caution that it must be done in stages, until the animals' own reflexive instincts take over and make the transition possible.

For instance, in being released into the wild, the animals are first put into a smaller enclosure, before they are released into a larger area of the reserve. Therefore the lion's encounter with the wild animal community is more gradual, and the transition is more successful. The expectation is that instinct will "kick in", and these animals will be able to sustain themselves with hunting skills that are inborn and instinctive. Supporters point out that South Africa is the only country in which the lion population is increasing, citing a growth of about 17 percent per year.

A distinction must be made between this type of lion program aimed at conservation, and the proliferation, particularly in the country of South Africa, of what are called "lion farms". These are "capture bred lions" raised to be shot by hunters in enclosed or fenced spaces. This is called the "canned lion" experience, in which tame lions are raised only to be killed by hunters. While legal in South Africa, the United States will not allow animals killed in this way to enter the country.

# About the Author

Dr. Diana Prince has a master's degree in English and a master's degree in philosophy from California State University at San Diego. She also has a PhD. in psychology from United States International University.

Printed in the United States
By Bookmasters